Chapter 1: Satoshi Nakamoto: The Enigmatic Creator

The Origins of Bitcoin

The origins of Bitcoin trace back to a pivotal moment in the financial landscape, marked by the release of Satoshi Nakamoto's white paper in October 2008. Titled "Bitcoin: A Peer-to-Peer Electronic Cash System," the document laid the groundwork for a decentralized currency that aimed to operate outside the control of traditional financial institutions. This was during a time of economic instability, particularly following the 2008 financial crisis, which fostered a widespread distrust in banks and centralized systems. The timing of Bitcoin's emergence was crucial, as it resonated with individuals seeking alternatives to the conventional financial system, setting the stage for a revolutionary change in how people viewed money and transactions.

The identity of Satoshi Nakamoto remains one of the most intriguing mysteries in the cryptocurrency world. The pseudonymous figure communicated primarily through online forums and email, engaging with early adopters and developers while maintaining an air of anonymity. Various theories have emerged regarding Nakamoto's true identity, ranging from individuals to groups of people, each with compelling arguments. Some believe Nakamoto is a computer scientist with a deep understanding of cryptography, while others speculate that the name represents a collective of developers disillusioned with the existing financial system. This ambiguity not only adds to the allure of Bitcoin but also speaks to the ethos of decentralization that underpins the cryptocurrency.

Satoshi's white paper was not just a technical document; it was a manifesto that challenged the status quo of monetary policy and financial governance. By proposing a system built on cryptographic proof instead of trust, Nakamoto introduced concepts that would later inspire a wave of cryptocurrencies and blockchain projects. The white paper articulated a vision of a decentralized currency that could facilitate peer-to-peer transactions without the need for intermediaries, effectively democratizing access to financial services. This foundational idea has since influenced countless innovations in the blockchain space, highlighting the profound impact of Nakamoto's work on the evolution of digital currencies.

The philosophical implications of Satoshi Nakamoto's anonymity extend beyond mere curiosity. The decision to remain unidentified was a conscious choice reflecting a broader philosophy of decentralization and individual sovereignty. By eschewing personal recognition, Nakamoto emphasized that Bitcoin was not about the individual but rather about the collective empowerment of users. This approach aligns with the principles of open-source technology, where the focus is on the community rather than a single entity. As Bitcoin grew in popularity, the discussions surrounding the importance of anonymity and privacy in financial transactions became increasingly relevant, influencing the development of subsequent cryptocurrencies that sought to prioritize user privacy.

In the years following Satoshi Nakamoto's departure from the public eye, Bitcoin has undergone significant evolution, shaping not only the cryptocurrency landscape but also broader discussions about finance and technology. The foundational ideals established by Nakamoto continue to inspire debates over regulation, governance, and ethical considerations in the blockchain space. As Bitcoin matures, the cultural impact of Nakamoto's vision remains palpable, evident in the growing acceptance of decentralized finance and the push for financial inclusion worldwide. The legacy of Satoshi Nakamoto is not merely that of a creator but as a catalyst for a global movement that challenges conventional financial norms and seeks to redefine the future of money.

The Creation of the White Paper

The creation of the white paper titled "Bitcoin: A Peer-to-Peer Electronic Cash System" marked a watershed moment in the landscape of digital finance and blockchain technology. Authored by the enigmatic Satoshi Nakamoto in 2008, the document laid the foundational principles of Bitcoin, outlining a decentralized digital currency that operates without a central authority. This white paper not only introduced the concept of cryptocurrency but also presented the underlying technology of blockchain, which would later revolutionize various sectors beyond finance. The clarity and precision of Nakamoto's writing provided a blueprint for a new financial paradigm that emphasized transparency, security, and autonomy.

In developing the white paper, Satoshi Nakamoto drew inspiration from a variety of existing technologies and concepts. The use of cryptographic techniques to secure transactions and control the creation of new units was central to the paper's design. Nakamoto referenced previous attempts at digital cash, highlighting limitations in their centralized structures, which often rendered them vulnerable to fraud and manipulation. This historical context served as a backdrop for the innovation presented in the white paper, which proposed a solution that combined elements of peer-to-peer networking with cryptographic security to enable direct transactions between users.

The impact of Satoshi's white paper on the cryptocurrency landscape was profound. It catalyzed the emergence of thousands of alternative cryptocurrencies and laid the groundwork for a burgeoning industry focused on blockchain technology. The white paper's concepts have been dissected, analyzed, and expanded upon by developers, investors, and enthusiasts alike, leading to an ongoing dialogue about the potential applications and implications of decentralized systems. As the first comprehensive framework for digital currency, the white paper encouraged a wave of innovation that continues to shape the financial world today.

Moreover, the anonymity of Satoshi Nakamoto plays a pivotal role in the narrative surrounding the white paper. The decision to remain faceless has sparked numerous theories about Nakamoto's identity, with speculation ranging from a lone genius to a collective of developers. This anonymity has not only contributed to the mystique of Bitcoin but also reinforced the philosophical underpinnings of decentralization. By eschewing personal identity, Nakamoto emphasized the importance of the technology itself over its creator, aligning with the core tenets of blockchain philosophy that advocate for distributed control and collective ownership.

Finally, the communication style and online presence of Satoshi Nakamoto further enriched the discourse surrounding the white paper and its implications. Engaging with early adopters and developers on forums such as Bitcointalk, Nakamoto fostered a community eager to explore the possibilities of the new technology. This engagement was characterized by a technical yet approachable tone, inviting collaboration and discussion. The legacy of the white paper, coupled with Nakamoto's deliberate anonymity and communication strategy, has left an indelible mark on the cultural and technological landscape, inspiring ongoing exploration of the ethical, legal, and social dimensions of decentralized finance.

The First Bitcoin Transaction

The first recorded transaction using Bitcoin occurred on January 12, 2009, and involved a transfer between Satoshi Nakamoto and a computer scientist named Hal Finney. This transaction is significant not only as a historical milestone but also as a demonstration of the practical application of the technology that Satoshi had introduced in his groundbreaking white paper, "Bitcoin: A Peer-to-Peer Electronic Cash System." Finney, who was one of the early adopters and supporters of Bitcoin, received ten bitcoins from Nakamoto, marking the beginning of a new financial era that would challenge traditional banking systems and redefine concepts of value and trust.

Satoshi's decision to initiate this transaction with Finney was not random; it underscored the collaborative spirit that is inherent in the cryptocurrency community. The transfer was executed on the Bitcoin network, which had just been launched with the release of version 0.1 of the Bitcoin software. This event set a precedent for what Bitcoin aimed to achieve: a decentralized currency that operates without the need for intermediaries. The simplicity of the transaction belied its revolutionary potential, as it showcased the feasibility of peer-to-peer transfers that bypass traditional financial institutions.

The ten bitcoins sent in this transaction would later become symbolic, representing both the beginning of a new digital currency and the profound shift in how individuals could transfer value. At the time, these bitcoins had negligible worth, but they would eventually appreciate dramatically in value, prompting discussions about the implications of cryptocurrency for investment and wealth distribution. This transaction not only marked the first of its kind but also ignited debates about the future of money, creating a ripple effect that would influence various sectors, including finance, technology, and legal frameworks.

In the broader context of Satoshi Nakamoto's legacy, this transaction highlighted the importance of trustlessness and anonymity in cryptocurrency. Nakamoto's choice to remain anonymous and communicate through online forums added an air of intrigue and allowed the focus to remain on the technology itself rather than the individual behind it. This anonymity has led to various theories regarding Satoshi's identity and has sparked discussions on the role of personal identity in the adoption of decentralized technologies. The transaction with Finney, conducted in this context, emphasized that the system was designed to function independently of its creator, aligning with the principles of decentralization that Satoshi championed.

As Bitcoin has evolved, the implications of that first transaction have become increasingly profound. It has paved the way for an entire ecosystem of cryptocurrencies and blockchain technologies, inspiring new innovations and applications across multiple industries. The initial act of transferring ten bitcoins has transformed into a broader conversation about the future of finance, the ethics of anonymity, and the potential for blockchain to reshape societal structures. This historical moment not only marks the inception of Bitcoin but also serves as a reminder of the transformative power of technology when combined with innovative thinking and a vision for a decentralized future.

Chapter 2: Theories on Satoshi Nakamoto's Identity

Leading Candidates

The search for Satoshi Nakamoto's identity has captivated the cryptocurrency community and the world at large since Bitcoin's inception. Various individuals and groups have emerged as leading candidates, each accompanied by their own theories and evidence. Among the most notable is Craig Wright, an Australian entrepreneur who has publicly claimed to be Satoshi. Wright's assertions have sparked a mix of intrigue and skepticism, as many in the cryptocurrency community question his credibility and the legitimacy of his evidence. His legal battles and public statements continue to fuel discussions about the true identity of Bitcoin's creator.

Another prominent candidate is Nick Szabo, a computer scientist and cryptographer known for his pioneering work on digital contracts and smart contracts before Bitcoin was created. Szabo's blog posts and writings on the concept of "bit gold," a precursor to Bitcoin, have led many to speculate that he could be Satoshi. His deep understanding of cryptography and economics aligns closely with the principles outlined in Bitcoin's white paper. However, Szabo has consistently denied being Nakamoto, stating that he values the anonymity of Bitcoin's founder.

Hal Finney, a well-respected developer and the first person to receive a Bitcoin transaction from Nakamoto, is also frequently mentioned as a leading candidate. Finney was an early adopter of Bitcoin and engaged with Nakamoto through email and forum discussions. His contributions to the development of Bitcoin and his familiarity with the technology have led some to believe that he may have played a significant role in its creation. Tragically, Finney passed away in 2014, but his legacy within the Bitcoin community remains influential.

Other candidates include individuals like Adam Back, the CEO of Blockstream and a cryptographic pioneer, and Dorian Nakamoto, a man who was mistakenly identified as Satoshi by a Newsweek article in 2014. Back's early work on hashcash, a proof-of-work system, demonstrates a technical foundation that resonates with Bitcoin's framework. Conversely, Dorian Nakamoto's claim of having no connection to Bitcoin, despite sharing a name with its creator, adds to the mystery surrounding Satoshi's identity. Each of these candidates brings a unique set of skills and experiences that could potentially align with the enigmatic figure of Nakamoto.

The ongoing debate over Satoshi Nakamoto's identity has profound implications for the cryptocurrency landscape. It raises questions about the nature of authorship, the significance of anonymity, and the philosophical principles underpinning decentralized systems. As the leading candidates are scrutinized and discussed, the legacy of Satoshi's work continues to influence the evolution of Bitcoin and the broader blockchain technology. Whether or not Satoshi's true identity is ever revealed, the impact of their vision will undoubtedly resonate throughout the world of finance and technology for years to come.

Analyzing the Evidence

The mystery surrounding Satoshi Nakamoto, the enigmatic creator of Bitcoin, continues to captivate researchers, enthusiasts, and casual observers alike. Analyzing the evidence related to Nakamoto's identity involves scrutinizing a variety of sources, including the original white paper, early forum posts, and insights from individuals who interacted with Satoshi during the inception of Bitcoin. This analysis is not merely an exercise in uncovering a name; it is essential for understanding the underlying philosophy that propelled the cryptocurrency movement and its implications for modern finance and technology.

The white paper titled "Bitcoin: A Peer-to-Peer Electronic Cash System" serves as a foundational document that outlines the principles of decentralized currency. Within its pages, Nakamoto articulates a vision for a financial system free from intermediaries, emphasizing the importance of trustlessness and transparency. The language and technical acumen displayed in the white paper have led to extensive analysis, with some theorists suggesting that they reflect a background in computer science and cryptography. Others propose that the writing style and choice of terminology may hint at Nakamoto's geographic or cultural background, though definitive conclusions remain elusive.

In exploring Satoshi's online presence, researchers have closely examined early communications in forums such as Bitcointalk and mailing lists. Nakamoto's interactions were characterized by a unique blend of technical expertise and philosophical inquiry, often emphasizing the importance of decentralization and individual empowerment. The tone of Satoshi's messages, which ranged from highly technical discussions to more casual exchanges, provides clues to the creator's identity, suggesting an individual who was not only knowledgeable but also deeply invested in the community's growth. This communication style fosters a connection with the ideals of the cryptocurrency movement, which values openness and collaboration.

Legal and ethical implications arise from Satoshi's anonymity, raising questions about accountability in the cryptocurrency space. This lack of a central figure challenges traditional notions of ownership and responsibility, complicating regulatory frameworks and fostering a culture of self-governance among cryptocurrency advocates. The absence of a visible leader means that the philosophy of decentralization is not merely theoretical; it has become a practical reality that influences how cryptocurrencies are developed and adopted. This scenario invites critical reflection on the balance between innovation and regulation, as well as the moral responsibilities of those involved in the ecosystem.

The cultural impact of Satoshi Nakamoto is evident in the way Bitcoin has transcended its initial purpose as a digital currency to become a symbol of resistance against established financial systems.

The mystery surrounding Satoshi has fueled narratives that celebrate the potential of decentralized technologies to empower individuals and challenge the status quo. As Bitcoin continues to evolve, the significance of Nakamoto's contributions remains a topic of ongoing debate, inspiring new generations of developers and thinkers to explore the possibilities of blockchain technology. The analysis of evidence related to Satoshi Nakamoto not only enriches our understanding of Bitcoin's origins but also underscores the broader implications of anonymity in the age of digital finance.

The Impact of Speculation

The phenomenon of speculation has profoundly influenced the landscape of cryptocurrency, particularly in relation to Bitcoin, the flagship digital currency introduced by Satoshi Nakamoto. Speculation refers to the act of buying and selling assets with the expectation of future price movements, and in the context of Bitcoin, it has led to dramatic fluctuations in value that are often disconnected from the underlying technology or utility of the cryptocurrency itself. This speculative environment has attracted a diverse range of participants, from seasoned investors to casual traders, each contributing to the volatility and unpredictability that characterize the market.

The impact of speculation on Bitcoin's price can be observed through various historical events that triggered significant market reactions. Following the release of Satoshi's white paper, Bitcoin initially experienced steady growth as early adopters and tech enthusiasts recognized its potential. However, as media coverage increased and more individuals became aware of Bitcoin, speculative trading began to dominate. The initial spikes in value were often driven by hype rather than fundamental developments, leading to bubbles that eventually burst, leaving many investors with substantial losses. These cycles of boom and bust have shaped the public perception of Bitcoin, often labeling it as a risky investment rather than a stable asset.

Moreover, speculation has not only influenced Bitcoin's price but has also affected its adoption and the broader cryptocurrency ecosystem. The speculative nature of the market has led to the emergence of numerous altcoins, many of which were created with the express purpose of capitalizing on the hype surrounding Bitcoin. While some of these projects have contributed to technological advancements and innovations within the blockchain space, others have been criticized for lacking a solid foundation, driven primarily by the desire for quick profits. This has raised questions about the legitimacy and sustainability of many cryptocurrencies, echoing Satoshi's original concerns about the integrity and security of a decentralized financial system.

Satoshi Nakamoto's anonymity plays a crucial role in the speculative nature of Bitcoin. The lack of a known identity creates an air of mystery that fuels speculation, as individuals and groups attempt to unravel the enigma surrounding Satoshi. This speculation extends beyond the identity itself; it influences market behavior, as traders often react to news and theories regarding Satoshi's actions or intentions. The ongoing speculation about Satoshi's holdings, estimated to be over a million bitcoins, also adds another layer of complexity, as the potential for such a large amount of bitcoin to enter the market could drastically affect supply and demand dynamics.

In conclusion, the impact of speculation on cryptocurrency cannot be understated. It has shaped Bitcoin's price trajectory, influenced the development of the broader crypto market, and created a culture of uncertainty and volatility. While speculation can drive innovation and interest in blockchain technology, it also poses risks that can undermine the foundational principles that Satoshi Nakamoto envisioned. Understanding the implications of speculation is essential for anyone looking to navigate the complex world of cryptocurrency, as it remains a defining characteristic of the market that continues to evolve alongside the technology itself.

Chapter 3: The Impact of Satoshi's White Paper on Cryptocurrency

Key Concepts Introduced

The subchapter "Key Concepts Introduced" delves into the foundational principles that Satoshi Nakamoto established, which have since shaped the landscape of cryptocurrency and blockchain technology. At the heart of these concepts is the notion of decentralization, which underpins the entire framework of Bitcoin. Satoshi envisioned a financial system where power was distributed among its users rather than concentrated in traditional institutions. This shift not only democratizes financial transactions but also enhances security and resilience against censorship and fraud, themes that resonate strongly in the context of today's digital economy.

Another pivotal concept introduced by Satoshi is the importance of trustless interactions. By utilizing cryptographic algorithms and a consensus mechanism, Satoshi designed a system where participants could engage in transactions without needing to establish trust in one another. This principle is crucial in a decentralized ecosystem where users can operate independently of third-party intermediaries. The implications of this idea extend beyond financial transactions, influencing various sectors, including supply chain management, voting systems, and digital identity verification.

Satoshi's white paper also introduced the concept of a distributed ledger, which serves as the backbone of blockchain technology. This ledger records all transactions in a manner that is transparent and immutable. Each block in the chain contains a cryptographic hash of the previous block, ensuring that any attempt to alter historical data is immediately detectable. This design not only enhances security but also fosters accountability within the network, as all participants can verify the integrity of the data without needing to trust a single entity.

The role of anonymity in Satoshi's philosophy also merits attention. By maintaining a pseudonymous identity, Satoshi emphasized the importance of privacy and security in the digital age. This decision raises pertinent questions about the legal and ethical implications of anonymity in technology. While it protects the creator from potential backlash and scrutiny, it also highlights the broader discussion about the balance between transparency and privacy in a rapidly evolving digital landscape.

Finally, Satoshi's communication style and online presence contributed significantly to the community's growth and ethos. Through forums, emails, and the original Bitcoin mailing list, Satoshi engaged with early adopters and developers, fostering a collaborative environment that encouraged innovation. This approach not only helped disseminate ideas but also built a sense of belonging among contributors. As Bitcoin has evolved post-Satoshi, these foundational concepts remain integral to understanding the ongoing development of cryptocurrency and the broader implications of blockchain technology in society.

The Reception of the White Paper

The reception of Satoshi Nakamoto's white paper, titled "Bitcoin: A Peer-to-Peer Electronic Cash System," marked a pivotal moment in the evolution of cryptocurrency and blockchain technology. Released in 2008, the white paper was initially met with skepticism from mainstream financial institutions and technology experts. Many viewed the concept of a decentralized digital currency as impractical, especially given the historical failures of earlier digital cash systems. However, as the foundational principles of Bitcoin began to resonate with a growing number of individuals disillusioned by traditional banking systems, the white paper gained traction. Early adopters and cryptography enthusiasts recognized its potential to challenge existing financial paradigms.

In the early days following its release, the white paper was circulated primarily within niche online communities. Forums dedicated to cryptography and alternative currencies became hotbeds of discussion and analysis. These platforms allowed for the dissemination of ideas and the critique of Satoshi's proposals. While some viewed Nakamoto's vision as revolutionary, others raised concerns about the feasibility and security of a decentralized currency. This dialogue laid the groundwork for a vibrant ecosystem of innovation and experimentation, driving early development efforts and the eventual launch of the Bitcoin network in January 2009.

Satoshi's white paper had an undeniable influence on the trajectory of cryptocurrency. It introduced concepts such as blockchain technology, decentralization, and cryptographic proof, which would become foundational elements for countless subsequent projects. As Bitcoin gained visibility, it inspired a wave of new cryptocurrencies and blockchain applications, each attempting to build upon or diverge from Nakamoto's original vision. The white paper not only served as a technical guide but also as a philosophical manifesto advocating for financial sovereignty and privacy, resonating with a demographic seeking alternatives to traditional monetary systems.

The anonymity of Satoshi Nakamoto further complicated the reception of the white paper. While some celebrated the decision to remain unseen, arguing that it allowed the focus to remain on the technology itself, others criticized it for lacking accountability. This duality reflects a broader debate within the cryptocurrency community regarding the role of anonymity in fostering innovation versus the need for trust in the development of financial systems. Satoshi's choice to remain anonymous has led to various theories about their identity, each attempting to understand the motivations and implications behind this enigmatic figure.

As the cryptocurrency landscape evolved, the initial skepticism surrounding Satoshi's white paper transformed into widespread recognition of its significance. Over time, Bitcoin's ascent to mainstream acceptance and the proliferation of blockchain technology underscored the profound impact of Nakamoto's ideas. The white paper not only catalyzed a financial revolution but also sparked discussions on decentralization, digital ownership, and the ethical implications of anonymity. In doing so, it cemented Satoshi Nakamoto's legacy as a pivotal figure in the history of technology and finance, influencing countless aspects of culture, economics, and governance in the digital age.

Influence on Future Cryptocurrencies

The influence of Satoshi Nakamoto on future cryptocurrencies is profound, shaping the landscape of digital currencies and blockchain technology in ways that continue to evolve. Satoshi's original vision, articulated in the Bitcoin white paper, laid the groundwork for an entire ecosystem of cryptocurrencies that emerged in the years following Bitcoin's inception. This foundational document not only introduced a revolutionary method for peer-to-peer transactions but also established principles such as decentralization, transparency, and security that have become hallmarks of subsequent projects. As new cryptocurrencies are developed, many look to Satoshi's work as a benchmark, attempting to either adhere to or diverge from the philosophies and technical frameworks he provided.

The theories surrounding Satoshi Nakamoto's identity have also contributed significantly to the discourse around future cryptocurrencies. The mystery of who Satoshi is—whether an individual or a group—has spurred speculation and intrigue, influencing how new projects position themselves in relation to Bitcoin. Some cryptocurrencies aim to build on the legacy of Satoshi by promoting similar values of decentralization and community governance, while others, in a bid to differentiate themselves, take more centralized approaches. This ongoing debate about Satoshi's identity and intentions continues to shape the narrative of cryptocurrency development and adoption.

Satoshi's white paper has not only inspired the creation of alternative cryptocurrencies but has also prompted discourse on the ethical and legal implications of anonymity in the blockchain space. Satoshi's choice to remain anonymous raises questions about accountability and the responsibilities of cryptocurrency creators. As new projects are launched, they often grapple with the balance between ensuring user privacy and maintaining transparency. This interplay has led to the emergence of various governance models and regulatory frameworks designed to address these challenges, influencing how future cryptocurrencies will operate within existing legal structures.

Furthermore, the evolution of Bitcoin post-Satoshi has set a precedent for the ongoing development of cryptocurrencies. As Bitcoin faced scaling issues and network congestion, new solutions such as layer-two technologies and alternative consensus mechanisms were proposed. These innovations have inspired a wave of new cryptocurrencies that seek to improve upon Bitcoin's shortcomings while still paying homage to its foundational principles. The lessons learned from Bitcoin's journey continue to guide developers as they create new digital assets, with many looking to strike a balance between innovation and the core tenets established by Satoshi.

Finally, the cultural impact of Satoshi Nakamoto on technology and finance cannot be understated. The ethos of decentralization and the democratization of currency have resonated with a diverse audience, leading to a vibrant community of developers, investors, and advocates. As new cryptocurrencies emerge, they often carry forward this cultural legacy, fostering a sense of belonging and collaboration among users. The ideologies and philosophies introduced by Satoshi have not only shaped the technical aspects of cryptocurrency but have also inspired a movement that challenges traditional financial systems, paving the way for a future where digital currencies play an integral role in global economies.

Chapter 4: Satoshi Nakamoto's Influence on Blockchain Technology

Innovations in Consensus Mechanisms

Innovations in consensus mechanisms have emerged as a critical area of development within the blockchain space, addressing challenges posed by traditional systems. Initially, Bitcoin's proof-of-work (PoW) mechanism laid the foundation for consensus, enabling decentralized validation of transactions. This mechanism, while effective in securing the network, has faced scrutiny for its environmental impact and energy consumption. As the cryptocurrency landscape has evolved, so too have the methods employed to achieve consensus, leading to the exploration of alternatives that promise greater efficiency and sustainability.

One notable innovation is the shift toward proof-of-stake (PoS) mechanisms, which allow participants to validate transactions based on the number of coins they hold and are willing to "stake" as collateral. This approach significantly reduces the energy requirements associated with mining, making it an attractive option for new blockchain projects seeking to mitigate their carbon footprints. Several prominent cryptocurrencies, including Ethereum, have begun transitioning to PoS, reflecting a broader industry trend toward more environmentally friendly consensus mechanisms. This evolution not only conserves energy but also enhances network security by reducing the risk of centralization associated with large mining operations.

In addition to PoS, other consensus mechanisms such as delegated proof-of-stake (DPoS) and practical Byzantine fault tolerance (PBFT) are gaining traction. DPoS introduces an element of democratic governance, where stakeholders elect delegates to validate transactions on their behalf, creating a more efficient and scalable system. Meanwhile, PBFT offers a solution to the Byzantine Generals Problem by ensuring that a consensus can be reached even when some nodes fail or act maliciously. These innovations highlight the ongoing efforts to refine consensus mechanisms, ultimately aiming to improve transaction speeds, reduce costs, and enhance overall network resilience.

The development of hybrid consensus models is another area where innovation is flourishing. These models combine elements of different consensus approaches, leveraging the strengths of each to create a more robust system. For instance, some projects utilize a combination of PoW and PoS to balance security and sustainability, while others incorporate mechanisms that allow for rapid consensus in specific scenarios, such as high-frequency trading. This flexibility enables blockchain networks to adapt to various use cases and user needs, showcasing the dynamic nature of consensus mechanism innovation.

As these innovations continue to shape the blockchain landscape, they also reflect the philosophical underpinnings laid out by Satoshi Nakamoto in the original Bitcoin white paper. The emphasis on decentralization, security, and efficiency remains central to the ongoing evolution of consensus mechanisms. By addressing the limitations of earlier models, these advancements not only honor Satoshi's vision but also pave the way for a more sustainable and inclusive cryptocurrency ecosystem. The exploration of new consensus mechanisms represents not just a technical progression but a response to the ethical and legal implications of blockchain technology, reinforcing the cultural impact of Satoshi Nakamoto's legacy on the tech and finance sectors.

Smart Contracts and Beyond

Smart contracts, a revolutionary application of blockchain technology, extend the capabilities of decentralized systems beyond mere currency transactions. These self-executing contracts, with the terms of the agreement directly written into code, eliminate the need for intermediaries, thereby reducing costs and increasing efficiency. Smart contracts encapsulate a trustless environment where parties can engage in transactions with the assurance that contractual obligations will be executed automatically when predetermined conditions are met. This innovation not only enhances security but also opens new avenues for various industries, from finance to supply chain management, fundamentally altering the traditional contract landscape.

The advent of smart contracts can be traced back to the foundational principles laid out in Satoshi Nakamoto's white paper. While the primary focus of Bitcoin was to create a decentralized digital currency, the underlying blockchain technology introduced a programmable layer that could support various applications. This capability has since evolved, with platforms like Ethereum enabling more complex and diverse smart contract functionalities. Such developments signify a shift from a singular focus on cryptocurrency to a broader perspective on blockchain's potential, showcasing how Satoshi's vision has inspired a myriad of innovations that transcend monetary transactions.

The influence of smart contracts has been profound, fostering a new wave of decentralized applications (dApps) that leverage blockchain's transparency and immutability. These dApps operate on networks governed by smart contracts, facilitating everything from decentralized finance (DeFi) to non-fungible tokens (NFTs). The ability for developers to create automated processes without the risk of manipulation or downtime presents a paradigm shift in how businesses and individuals interact. This approach not only democratizes access to technology but also empowers users by reducing reliance on centralized authorities, aligning closely with Satoshi's original ideals of decentralization and autonomy.

However, the rise of smart contracts also brings forth legal and ethical considerations that warrant careful examination. The anonymity of Satoshi Nakamoto, coupled with the pseudonymous nature of blockchain transactions, raises questions about accountability and regulatory oversight. As smart contracts operate independently of traditional legal frameworks, issues surrounding enforceability, jurisdiction, and dispute resolution become increasingly complex. The challenge lies in balancing the innovative potential of these technologies with the need for a robust legal framework that protects users without stifling innovation.

Looking ahead, the evolution of smart contracts is poised to influence various sectors, driving advancements in automation and decentralized governance. As blockchain technology continues to mature, the integration of smart contracts into everyday applications will likely become more prevalent, transforming industries in ways we are only beginning to understand. Satoshi Nakamoto's initial vision has sparked an ongoing journey, one that not only honors the principles of decentralization but also invites a broader dialogue on the ethical implications and societal impacts of these groundbreaking technologies. The future of smart contracts and blockchain offers a canvas for innovation that remains true to the spirit of Satoshi's legacy.

The Rise of Decentralized Applications

The rise of decentralized applications (dApps) represents a significant evolution in the landscape of blockchain technology, building on the foundational principles set forth by Satoshi Nakamoto in the Bitcoin white paper. At its core, a decentralized application operates on a peer-to-peer network rather than being hosted on centralized servers. This shift enables greater transparency, security, and user control over data, which are fundamental tenets that Nakamoto advocated for in creating Bitcoin. The emergence of dApps marks a pivotal moment in the ongoing quest for decentralization, pushing the boundaries of what blockchain technology can achieve beyond mere digital currency.

The development of Ethereum in 2015 catalyzed the growth of decentralized applications by introducing smart contracts, self-executing agreements coded onto the blockchain. This innovation allowed developers to create complex applications that could operate autonomously, further enhancing the appeal of decentralization. Unlike Bitcoin, which primarily serves as a digital currency, Ethereum provided a versatile platform for building a wide array of dApps across various industries, from finance to gaming. This flexibility has led to a surge in interest and investment in dApps, as they offer unique solutions to traditional problems in sectors such as supply chain management, healthcare, and identity verification.

As dApps continue to proliferate, they embody the ethos of Satoshi Nakamoto's vision of removing intermediaries from financial transactions and fostering a more equitable system. The decentralized nature of these applications helps to mitigate risks associated with central points of failure, such as data breaches and censorship. By distributing control among users, dApps create an environment where individuals can engage with technology and each other without the need for trusted third parties. This shift not only empowers users but also aligns with the growing demand for privacy and autonomy in an increasingly digital world.

Additionally, the rise of decentralized finance (DeFi) exemplifies the transformative potential of dApps. DeFi platforms allow users to lend, borrow, and trade assets without the oversight of traditional financial institutions. This movement challenges the status quo of finance, echoing Satoshi's critique of centralized banking systems and the inherent inefficiencies they introduce. By leveraging smart contracts and blockchain technology, DeFi applications democratize access to financial services, enabling individuals across the globe, particularly in underbanked regions, to participate in the economy in unprecedented ways.

However, the ascent of decentralized applications also raises important legal and ethical questions. As dApps operate outside conventional regulatory frameworks, issues such as user protection, compliance, and accountability become increasingly complex. The anonymity that often accompanies blockchain technology, reminiscent of Satoshi Nakamoto's own obscured identity, complicates the landscape further. While the philosophy of decentralization champions the freedom and empowerment of individuals, it also necessitates a dialogue on the implications of such freedom in a world where digital interactions can remain largely untraceable. As the ecosystem of dApps continues to mature, stakeholders must grapple with the dualities of innovation and regulation, ensuring that the legacy of Satoshi Nakamoto guides the ethical development of this transformative technology.

Chapter 5: The Role of Anonymity in Satoshi's Philosophy

The Importance of Privacy

The importance of privacy in the realm of cryptocurrency cannot be overstated, particularly when examining the foundational principles laid out by Satoshi Nakamoto. Privacy serves as a cornerstone of the blockchain philosophy, promoting individual autonomy and safeguarding personal data from invasive surveillance. In a world where digital footprints are increasingly monitored, the ability to conduct transactions without revealing one's identity resonates deeply with concerns over government overreach and corporate data exploitation. Satoshi's vision encompassed not only a decentralized financial system but also a framework that inherently protects users from the prying eyes of third parties.

By introducing the pseudonymous nature of Bitcoin, Satoshi Nakamoto emphasized the value of anonymity in financial transactions. This anonymity is significant in ensuring that users can engage freely in economic activities without fear of retribution or judgment. The notion of a digital currency that doesn't require personal identification aligned with Satoshi's ideals of privacy and independence. This foundational aspect has influenced the development of various cryptocurrencies that prioritize privacy, leading to an ongoing discourse about the balance between transparency and confidentiality in blockchain systems.

Moreover, privacy is intrinsically linked to the concept of decentralization, which Satoshi championed as a means to empower individuals. Decentralization diminishes the control held by centralized authorities, thereby enhancing user privacy. In Satoshi's framework, the removal of intermediaries not only streamlines transactions but also protects users from potential data breaches and misuse of information. The evolution of Bitcoin and other cryptocurrencies reflects an ongoing commitment to these principles, as developers continuously explore ways to bolster privacy features while maintaining the integrity of the blockchain.

The legal and ethical implications surrounding Satoshi's anonymity further underscore the importance of privacy in cryptocurrency. While anonymity can facilitate illicit activities, it also serves as a necessary shield for those seeking to escape oppressive regimes or avoid unwarranted scrutiny. Satoshi's decision to remain unidentified raises questions about the responsibilities and rights of creators in the digital age. The conversation around privacy is not merely about protecting individual users but also about fostering an environment where innovation can thrive without the constraints of excessive oversight.

Finally, the cultural impact of Satoshi Nakamoto's work extends into broader societal discussions about privacy and security in a digital world. As individuals become more aware of the implications of data sharing, the principles laid out in Satoshi's white paper resonate with a growing demand for privacy-preserving technologies. The cryptocurrency movement, inspired by Satoshi, has sparked a reevaluation of privacy norms in finance and technology, encouraging a shift towards systems that prioritize user sovereignty. This ongoing dialogue highlights the critical role of privacy in shaping the future of not only cryptocurrency but also the broader landscape of digital interactions.

Anonymity vs. Transparency

Anonymity and transparency are two pivotal concepts that have shaped the narrative surrounding Bitcoin and its enigmatic creator, Satoshi Nakamoto. The decision to remain anonymous has sparked extensive debate within the cryptocurrency community, influencing how Bitcoin is perceived and adopted. Satoshi's choice to withhold personal identity not only exemplifies a commitment to the principles of decentralization but also raises critical questions regarding trust, accountability, and the broader implications for the cryptocurrency ecosystem. This duality of anonymity versus transparency reflects the underlying ethos of blockchain technology and challenges traditional paradigms of financial systems and governance.

At the core of Satoshi Nakamoto's philosophy is the belief that trust should not be placed in individuals but rather in the technology itself. By remaining anonymous, Satoshi effectively decentralizes authority, allowing users to engage with the network without the influence of a central figure. This approach aligns with the foundational principles of blockchain, which prioritize collective consensus over individual power. The anonymity of Satoshi invites users to focus on the protocol's integrity and the decentralized nature of the network, rather than the personality or motives of its creator. This shift in focus is crucial in fostering a community-driven ecosystem where innovation can thrive without the constraints of hierarchical structures.

Conversely, the lack of transparency surrounding Satoshi's identity invites skepticism and speculation. Various theories surrounding Satoshi Nakamoto's true identity often divert attention from the technological advancements and the transformative potential of Bitcoin itself. As discussions about Satoshi's identity proliferate, they can overshadow critical dialogues regarding blockchain technology's impact on finance and society. This phenomenon illustrates a paradox where the very anonymity that protects Satoshi's vision also complicates the narrative, leading to fragmented interpretations of Bitcoin's purpose and value.

The implications of anonymity extend beyond Satoshi's identity to the broader legal and ethical landscape of cryptocurrency. As governments and regulatory bodies grapple with the challenges presented by decentralized systems, the need for transparency becomes increasingly apparent. While anonymity can protect users from surveillance and censorship, it can also facilitate illicit activities, raising concerns about the potential for misuse. This tension between the desire for privacy and the need for accountability is a central theme in the ongoing discussions surrounding cryptocurrency regulation, compelling stakeholders to consider the balance between these competing interests.

Ultimately, the discussion of anonymity versus transparency in the context of Satoshi Nakamoto serves as a microcosm of the larger debates within the cryptocurrency landscape. It highlights the challenges of fostering innovation while ensuring security and trust in a decentralized system. As the cryptocurrency space continues to evolve, the enduring legacy of Satoshi will likely inform future developments, shaping how anonymity and transparency are navigated in the pursuit of a decentralized financial future. Understanding this dynamic is essential for anyone engaged in the cryptocurrency community, as it lays the groundwork for addressing the ethical, legal, and cultural implications of Satoshi's choices and their lasting influence on blockchain technology.

Anonymity in the Context of Trust

Anonymity plays a critical role in the context of trust within the cryptocurrency ecosystem, particularly in relation to Satoshi Nakamoto, the enigmatic figure behind Bitcoin's inception. Satoshi's decision to remain anonymous not only influenced the perception of Bitcoin but also shaped the underlying principles of trust in decentralized systems. By withholding their identity, Satoshi positioned Bitcoin as a collective effort rather than a product of a single individual, fostering a sense of community ownership and shared purpose among its users. This anonymity invites users to place trust in the technology itself, rather than in any single person or authority.

The implications of Satoshi's anonymity extend beyond mere personal identity; they resonate deeply with the philosophical foundations of the cryptocurrency movement. Trust in Bitcoin does not derive from a centralized authority or a recognizable leader; instead, it stems from the blockchain's immutable ledger and the consensus mechanism that governs it. This decentralized trust model challenges traditional financial systems, where trust is often placed in institutions and individuals. By creating a system that functions independently of any identifiable leader, Satoshi promoted a new paradigm in which trust is distributed among participants, enhancing the resilience and reliability of the network.

Moreover, Satoshi's anonymity raises important questions about the ethical and legal ramifications of such a choice. While some argue that anonymity is essential for protecting the creator from potential backlash or legal repercussions, others contend that it obscures accountability. This lack of identifiable leadership can lead to challenges in governance and regulation, as users may find it difficult to address grievances or seek redress in cases of fraud or malfunction. The debate surrounding Satoshi's anonymity highlights a broader tension in the cryptocurrency space between the ideals of freedom and the need for responsible stewardship of the technology.

Satoshi's communication style and online presence further complicate the narrative surrounding anonymity and trust. Through a series of forum posts and emails, Satoshi articulated a vision for a decentralized financial system that resonates with many today. The clarity and precision of Satoshi's writings instilled confidence in the project, demonstrating that even without a physical identity, strong ideas could cultivate trust. This paradox emphasizes that while anonymity can obscure the creator, it can simultaneously empower the message and the technology, encouraging users to engage with the ideas rather than the person behind them.

In the historical context of Bitcoin's creation, Satoshi's anonymity has also influenced the evolution of the cryptocurrency landscape. As new projects emerge and the community grows, the foundational principles laid down by Satoshi continue to inform discussions about trust, decentralization, and governance. The legacy of Satoshi Nakamoto serves as a reminder that in a world where traditional notions of trust are increasingly questioned, anonymity can be both a shield and a catalyst for innovation. It challenges us to rethink how trust is constructed in digital spaces and encourages a collective approach to building systems that prioritize transparency, security, and user empowerment.

Chapter 6: Satoshi Nakamoto's Communication Style and Online Presence

Forums and Early Discussions

Forums and early discussions played a crucial role in the conceptualization and initial adoption of Bitcoin, serving as the breeding ground for ideas, debates, and community building. In the formative years of cryptocurrency, platforms such as Bitcointalk.org became central hubs where enthusiasts, developers, and skeptics gathered to discuss the implications of Satoshi Nakamoto's white paper. These discussions provided a space for users to share insights, propose improvements, and address concerns regarding the nascent technology. The significance of these forums cannot be understated, as they not only shaped the technical evolution of Bitcoin but also fostered a sense of community among early adopters.

Satoshi Nakamoto's communication style was characterized by clarity and precision, which resonated well with the community. His posts often sparked in-depth discussions that revealed both the potential and limitations of the technology. Participants in these forums debated various aspects of Bitcoin, from its technical specifications to its philosophical underpinnings regarding decentralization and anonymity. The engagement in these discussions contributed to the formation of a collective understanding of Bitcoin, allowing participants to collaboratively refine their ideas about what cryptocurrency could achieve in the broader context of finance and society.

The anonymity of Satoshi Nakamoto also played a pivotal role in shaping the community's culture and ethos. By choosing to remain unidentified, Satoshi not only emphasized the importance of the technology over the individual but also invited speculation and intrigue regarding his identity. The mystery surrounding Satoshi spurred numerous theories, which became a topic of discussion in various forums. This anonymity fostered a sense of egalitarianism within the community, where ideas were judged on merit rather than the status of the contributor. As debates raged over Satoshi's identity, the focus remained on the principles of decentralization and the potential impact of Bitcoin on the existing financial system.

The discussions that unfolded in these early forums laid the groundwork for a rich tapestry of ideas that would influence the trajectory of Bitcoin and subsequent cryptocurrencies. Participants brainstormed potential use cases, addressed security concerns, and explored the ethical implications of a decentralized currency. These conversations not only highlighted the community's enthusiasm but also revealed a shared commitment to creating a financial system that could operate independently of traditional institutions. In this way, the forums acted as incubators for innovation, ensuring that diverse perspectives contributed to the evolution of Bitcoin.

As Bitcoin began to gain traction, the discussions in these early forums evolved to include critiques and analyses of its impact on the broader economic landscape. Participants examined the legal implications of Satoshi's anonymity and the ethical considerations surrounding the technology's potential to disrupt established financial systems. The forums became a space for reflection on the cultural impact of Satoshi Nakamoto, as the community grappled with the transformative power of blockchain technology. Ultimately, these early discussions not only paved the way for future developments in the cryptocurrency space but also cemented the legacy of Satoshi Nakamoto as a pivotal figure in the ongoing narrative of digital finance.

The Language of Satoshi

The language of Satoshi Nakamoto, the enigmatic figure behind Bitcoin, is characterized by clarity, precision, and an underlying philosophical depth that has captivated audiences since the release of the Bitcoin white paper in 2008. Satoshi's writing style reflects a profound understanding of both technical concepts and human behavior, merging them into a compelling narrative about the potential for a decentralized digital currency. The white paper itself is a masterclass in succinctness, outlining complex ideas in a manner that is accessible yet intellectually rigorous, allowing readers from various backgrounds to grasp the potential of blockchain technology.

In Satoshi's communications, whether in forum posts or emails, there is a consistent emphasis on decentralization and the empowerment of individuals through technology. This focus is not merely technical; it embodies a palpable belief in the values of freedom, privacy, and autonomy. Satoshi's choice of language often evokes a sense of urgency and purpose, urging the community to consider the implications of a financial system that operates outside traditional institutions. This philosophical underpinning has resonated strongly with those disillusioned by centralized financial systems, reinforcing the cultural and ideological significance of Bitcoin.

Satoshi's anonymity adds another layer to the language employed in their writings. By remaining faceless, Satoshi effectively shifts the focus from the individual to the ideas themselves, promoting a community-driven ethos that is central to the philosophy of cryptocurrency. This intentional obscurity fosters a unique dynamic in which the community can engage with the ideas without the influence of a singular authoritative figure. The language of Satoshi, therefore, becomes a tool for empowerment, encouraging collaboration and innovation while simultaneously challenging the status quo.

The historical context in which Satoshi communicated further enriches the understanding of their language. Emerging from the 2008 financial crisis, Satoshi's writings tapped into a collective anxiety about the stability of traditional financial systems and the potential for technology to offer solutions. The language reflects a nuanced understanding of the socio-economic landscape, combining technical expertise with a profound awareness of the societal implications of financial systems. This context not only demonstrates Satoshi's foresight but also illustrates the cultural impact that the language of Satoshi has had on the tech and finance sectors.

As Bitcoin evolved post-Satoshi, the language and concepts introduced by Nakamoto continued to shape discussions surrounding cryptocurrency and blockchain technology. Satoshi's influence is seen in the ongoing debates about decentralization, the ethical implications of anonymity, and the cultural shifts within finance. The legacy of Satoshi's language serves as a foundation for ongoing dialogue, inspiring new generations of developers, investors, and enthusiasts to engage with the transformative potential of blockchain technology while remaining rooted in the original principles articulated by its creator.

Engagement with the Community

Engagement with the community has been a cornerstone of the cryptocurrency movement since the inception of Bitcoin. Satoshi Nakamoto, the enigmatic creator, understood that for Bitcoin to thrive, it would require the active participation and support of a diverse group of individuals. This engagement was not merely a strategy for adoption but a philosophical underpinning that emphasized the importance of decentralization and collective ownership. Satoshi's approach fostered a sense of belonging among early adopters, encouraging them to contribute to the development and governance of the network.

The creation of forums and online platforms for discussion played a significant role in building a community around Bitcoin. Satoshi regularly communicated with users through mailing lists and forums, sharing insights, addressing concerns, and soliciting feedback. This two-way communication not only helped refine the technology but also cultivated a culture of transparency and collaboration. The open-source nature of Bitcoin allowed developers and enthusiasts alike to engage with the code, suggest improvements, and participate in the evolution of the project, creating a robust ecosystem of contributors who were invested in its success.

Satoshi's white paper, "Bitcoin: A Peer-to-Peer Electronic Cash System," served as a foundational document that sparked widespread interest and discussion among cryptographers, software developers, and financial theorists. By outlining a vision for a decentralized currency free from government control, Satoshi ignited a movement that challenged traditional financial systems. The community's engagement with this vision led to numerous discussions on the implications of such a currency, influencing the direction of subsequent projects and fostering a culture of innovation within the cryptocurrency space.

Moreover, the anonymity of Satoshi Nakamoto has had a profound impact on community dynamics and engagement. This choice of anonymity has prompted extensive theories regarding Satoshi's identity, leading to debates that have fueled interest in Bitcoin and its underlying principles. The mystery surrounding Satoshi serves as a catalyst for community engagement, as individuals attempt to uncover the truth while simultaneously grappling with the philosophical implications of anonymity in a digital age. This ongoing dialogue reflects a deep-seated interest in the values that Satoshi represented, including privacy, empowerment, and the rejection of centralized authority.

As Bitcoin evolved post-Satoshi, the community continued to play a crucial role in shaping its trajectory. Developers, miners, and users have collaborated to address challenges such as scalability, security, and regulatory issues. The ongoing engagement of this community has been instrumental in navigating the complexities of a rapidly changing landscape. By fostering an inclusive environment where diverse perspectives are welcomed, the cryptocurrency community has not only sustained Satoshi's legacy but also expanded upon it, ensuring that the ideals of decentralization and innovation remain at the forefront of its mission.

Chapter 7: Historical Context of Bitcoin's Creation

The Financial Crisis of 2008

The financial crisis of 2008 marked a pivotal moment in global economic history, exposing vulnerabilities within financial systems and prompting widespread disillusionment with traditional banking practices. As the crisis unfolded, millions lost their jobs, homes, and savings, leading to a profound questioning of the economic models that had governed the financial landscape. This turmoil created fertile ground for the emergence of alternative financial systems, ultimately paving the way for Bitcoin and the philosophy underpinning its creation.

The crisis was largely precipitated by the collapse of the housing market, fueled by subprime mortgage lending and risky financial instruments like mortgage-backed securities. As banks failed and government bailouts became necessary to stabilize the economy, the public's trust in centralized financial institutions eroded. This environment of skepticism and fear highlighted the need for a more resilient and transparent form of currency that could operate outside the control of traditional financial systems. Satoshi Nakamoto's vision of Bitcoin as a decentralized, peer-to-peer currency directly responded to this need for an alternative.

Satoshi's white paper, released in October 2008, articulated a revolutionary approach to money that emphasized decentralization and security. By leveraging blockchain technology, Bitcoin offered a solution to the problems of trust and transparency that had been highlighted during the financial crisis. The white paper not only detailed the technical workings of Bitcoin but also posited a new economic philosophy that challenged the established norms of financial governance. This document became the foundation of a movement that sought to restore financial autonomy to individuals, free from the constraints of traditional banks.

In the aftermath of the crisis, Bitcoin began to attract attention as an innovative solution to the shortcomings of existing financial systems. The anonymity of Satoshi Nakamoto, combined with the decentralized nature of Bitcoin, appealed to those disillusioned by the failures of centralized institutions. Satoshi's communication style, marked by concise and thoughtful contributions to online forums, further cultivated a sense of community and purpose among early adopters. This period saw a growing interest in the principles of decentralization, which became central to the identity of Bitcoin and the broader cryptocurrency ecosystem.

The cultural impact of Satoshi Nakamoto's creation extended beyond mere financial transactions; it ignited discussions around legal and ethical implications of anonymity in the digital age. As Bitcoin evolved post-Satoshi, the principles of decentralization and the quest for a transparent monetary system influenced various sectors, including finance, technology, and governance. The legacy of the 2008 financial crisis continues to resonate, as the ideals encapsulated in Satoshi's work inspire ongoing innovations in blockchain technology and alternative currencies, shaping the future of how society engages with money and value.

Technological Innovations Leading to Bitcoin

The emergence of Bitcoin was not an isolated event but rather the culmination of various technological innovations that set the stage for its development. Key among these innovations was the advent of cryptographic techniques that allowed for secure communication and data integrity. Public key cryptography, for instance, enabled users to exchange information and currency securely without the need for a central authority. This was essential in establishing trust in a decentralized digital currency system, where participants could engage in transactions without relying on traditional banking institutions.

Another significant technological advancement was the rise of peer-to-peer networking. This framework facilitated the direct exchange of data between users, laying the groundwork for Bitcoin's decentralized architecture. By allowing individuals to connect directly with one another, peer-to-peer networks eliminated the need for intermediaries, which was a fundamental principle that Satoshi Nakamoto embraced. This innovation not only supported the idea of a decentralized currency but also enhanced the resilience of the system against censorship and control by any single entity.

Blockchain technology itself emerged as a revolutionary method of recording transactions. The concept of a distributed ledger, where each participant maintains a copy of the entire history of transactions, ensured transparency and security. Satoshi's white paper introduced the idea of a blockchain that timestamps transactions and links them in a secure manner, making it nearly impossible to alter the history of transactions without detection. This innovation was crucial in addressing the double-spending problem that plagued digital currencies, providing a robust solution that Bitcoin would capitalize on.

The rise of open-source software also played a vital role in the development of Bitcoin. By leveraging open-source principles, Satoshi Nakamoto encouraged collaboration and innovation among developers, allowing anyone to contribute to the project. This not only fostered a community around Bitcoin but also ensured that the code underwent rigorous scrutiny, enhancing its security and reliability. The open-source model became a defining characteristic of the cryptocurrency movement, promoting transparency and trust within the ecosystem.

Lastly, advancements in computing power and storage capacity were instrumental in making Bitcoin a feasible reality. As personal computers became more powerful and accessible, the ability to run full nodes and mine Bitcoin became attainable for more individuals. This democratization of technology aligned perfectly with Satoshi's vision of a decentralized currency, empowering users to participate in the network and contribute to its security. Together, these technological innovations created a fertile ground for Bitcoin's inception, marking a significant milestone in the evolution of digital currency and blockchain technology.

The Influence of Cypherpunk Ideology

The cypherpunk ideology has significantly influenced the development of Bitcoin and blockchain technology, weaving itself into the very fabric of Satoshi Nakamoto's vision. At its core, cypherpunk philosophy advocates for privacy, individual freedom, and the use of cryptography as a means to achieve these goals. This movement emerged in the late 1980s and early 1990s, fueled by concerns over government surveillance and the erosion of personal liberties. By integrating these principles into Bitcoin, Satoshi not only created a digital currency but also a manifesto for a new financial paradigm focused on autonomy and privacy.

Satoshi's white paper, "Bitcoin: A Peer-to-Peer Electronic Cash System," reflects the cypherpunk ethos through its emphasis on decentralization and trustless transactions. The design of Bitcoin eliminates the need for intermediaries, empowering users to engage in direct transactions without relying on traditional financial institutions. This approach aligns with cypherpunk beliefs, which value the empowerment of individuals over centralized authorities. By crafting a system where users can maintain their financial privacy while participating in a transparent ledger, Satoshi effectively bridged the ideals of the cypherpunk movement with practical technology.

Moreover, the anonymity of Satoshi Nakamoto is a critical element that resonates with cypherpunk values. The decision to remain pseudonymous underscores the belief that privacy is paramount, especially in an age where surveillance is pervasive. Satoshi's choice to separate their identity from the creation of Bitcoin echoes the cypherpunk warning against the encroachment of state power and the importance of maintaining individual sovereignty. This anonymity has also sparked numerous theories surrounding Satoshi's identity, reinforcing the notion that the principles behind Bitcoin are more significant than any single individual.

The historical context of Bitcoin's creation is steeped in the concerns and aspirations of the cypherpunk community. During a time when financial systems faced increasing instability, Satoshi's innovation emerged as a direct response to the failures of traditional banking and the desire for a more secure and private means of conducting transactions. The cypherpunk ideology provided the philosophical underpinning for Bitcoin, encouraging a generation of technologists and activists to rethink the future of money and personal freedom. This backdrop highlights the ongoing relevance of cypherpunk beliefs in shaping the evolving landscape of blockchain technology.

As Bitcoin has evolved post-Satoshi, the influence of cypherpunk ideology continues to manifest in various facets of the cryptocurrency ecosystem. The push for privacy-focused coins, decentralized exchanges, and smart contracts reflects a sustained commitment to the cypherpunk principles of autonomy and cryptographic security. Furthermore, the ongoing discourse surrounding legal and ethical implications of Satoshi's anonymity highlights the tension between innovation and regulation. Ultimately, the legacy of cypherpunk thought remains integral to understanding the motivations behind Bitcoin's creation and its potential to redefine societal norms around finance and personal freedom.

Chapter 8: The Evolution of Bitcoin Post-Satoshi

Key Developments After Satoshi's Departure

The period following Satoshi Nakamoto's departure from the public eye in late 2010 marked a significant turning point in the evolution of Bitcoin and the broader cryptocurrency landscape. As the original creator of Bitcoin, Satoshi's absence left a notable vacuum that prompted the community to rally around the principles enshrined in the Bitcoin white paper. This shift catalyzed the emergence of prominent figures and organizations that would take on leadership roles, fostering a collaborative environment that encouraged innovation while upholding Satoshi's foundational ideals of decentralization and trustless transactions.

One of the most critical developments post-Satoshi was the formation of key software development teams and communities dedicated to maintaining and enhancing the Bitcoin protocol. Developers like Gavin Andresen and groups such as Bitcoin Core became instrumental in managing updates and implementing improvements. The transition from Satoshi's direct oversight to a more decentralized model of governance illustrated the community's commitment to Satoshi's vision. This shift allowed for diverse input from various stakeholders, making Bitcoin a more robust and resilient network capable of adapting to the challenges of a fast-evolving technological landscape.

Additionally, the increase in speculation and investment in Bitcoin following Satoshi's exit underscored the growing interest in cryptocurrencies. As Bitcoin gained traction, new exchanges emerged, enabling broader access to trading and investment opportunities. The price volatility that characterized this period attracted both retail and institutional investors, contributing to Bitcoin's narrative as "digital gold." This rise in value prompted discussions about the legal and regulatory implications of cryptocurrencies, leading to greater scrutiny from governments and financial institutions worldwide.

The cultural impact of Satoshi Nakamoto's anonymity also became increasingly relevant in the post-Satoshi era. The mystery surrounding Satoshi's identity fostered a sense of intrigue and speculation that permeated discussions within the cryptocurrency community. Various theories about Satoshi's identity circulated, reflecting a broader fascination with the figure who initiated a technological revolution. This ambiguity reinforced the ideals of decentralization, as the focus shifted from a singular creator to the collective contributions of countless developers, enthusiasts, and users, embodying the spirit of a truly decentralized network.

Finally, Satoshi's philosophical approach to anonymity influenced the ethical discourse within the cryptocurrency space. The decision to remain anonymous prompted discussions about privacy, data ownership, and the ethical implications of blockchain technology. This emphasis on anonymity resonated with many users who valued the potential for financial sovereignty and personal privacy in an increasingly surveillance-driven world. The values articulated by Satoshi continue to shape the trajectory of blockchain technology and its applications, highlighting the enduring legacy of Bitcoin and the principles of decentralization that Satoshi championed.

The Role of Developers and the Community

The role of developers and the community in the evolution of blockchain technology and cryptocurrency is a critical aspect that reflects the foundational principles laid out by Satoshi Nakamoto. While Satoshi's initial vision materialized through the white paper and the first Bitcoin software, it is the ongoing contributions from developers and the surrounding community that have propelled the technology forward. These individuals and groups have not only enhanced the functionality and security of the network but have also ensured that the ideals of decentralization and democratization remain central to the cryptocurrency movement.

Developers play a pivotal role in the ongoing maintenance and improvement of blockchain protocols. They are responsible for writing code, fixing bugs, and implementing updates that enhance the security and efficiency of the network. The open-source nature of Bitcoin and other cryptocurrencies allows developers from around the world to contribute to the codebase, fostering a collaborative environment that aligns with Satoshi's vision of a decentralized financial system. This community-driven approach helps mitigate risks associated with centralized control, as decisions regarding the development of the protocol are made collectively rather than dictated by a single entity.

The community surrounding cryptocurrency serves as a vital support system that drives adoption and innovation. This includes not only developers but also users, miners, investors, and enthusiasts who contribute to discussions, share knowledge, and promote the technology. Online forums, social media platforms, and meetups are common venues where community members exchange ideas and collaborate on projects. This vibrant ecosystem helps to educate new users about the benefits and challenges of cryptocurrency, while also fostering a culture of transparency and accountability within the space.

Moreover, the community has a significant influence on the democratic processes that govern the evolution of blockchain technology. Through mechanisms such as Bitcoin Improvement Proposals (BIPs), community members can propose changes or enhancements to the protocol. The discussion and voting processes that follow are examples of how decentralized governance can operate in practice, echoing Satoshi's original intent to create a system free from centralized authority. This participatory model empowers users and developers alike, ensuring that the technology evolves in a manner that reflects the collective interests of its stakeholders.

In conclusion, the interplay between developers and the community is essential to the ongoing legacy of Satoshi Nakamoto's vision. By fostering a collaborative environment that encourages innovation and inclusivity, the cryptocurrency community continues to uphold the principles of decentralization and transparency. As the landscape of blockchain technology evolves, the contributions of developers and the engagement of the community will remain critical in shaping its future, ensuring that Satoshi's legacy endures and adapts to the challenges of a rapidly changing world.

Market Dynamics and Adoption

Market dynamics surrounding cryptocurrency are heavily influenced by the foundational principles established by Satoshi Nakamoto. The initial release of the Bitcoin white paper in 2008 set in motion a series of events that would alter the landscape of finance and technology. The principles of decentralization, transparency, and security resonated with early adopters, creating an enthusiastic community eager to embrace these revolutionary concepts. As Bitcoin started gaining traction, the market dynamics shifted from niche interest to broader acceptance, driven by a combination of technological advancements, economic factors, and social movements advocating for financial independence.

Adoption of cryptocurrency has evolved through various phases, often mirroring broader technological adoption trends. The early days saw a small group of enthusiasts and developers engaging with Bitcoin, primarily motivated by ideological beliefs in decentralization and a distrust of traditional financial institutions. As the technology matured and more use cases emerged, particularly with the rise of altcoins and decentralized applications, the user base expanded. This shift was further facilitated by educational efforts and increased media coverage, which raised awareness about the potential benefits of blockchain technology beyond mere currency speculation.

The influence of Satoshi Nakamoto's anonymity cannot be overstated in the context of market dynamics. By choosing to remain an elusive figure, Nakamoto positioned Bitcoin as a decentralized currency free from the influence of any single entity or government.

This choice has fostered a sense of community ownership and responsibility among users, driving grassroots movements that advocate for greater adoption. The mystery surrounding Nakamoto's identity has also created a narrative that attracts media attention, fueling public interest and speculation, and contributing to the cryptocurrency's volatility and market behavior.

The interplay between technological advancement and market forces continues to shape the adoption of cryptocurrency. Innovations such as the Lightning Network and smart contracts have enhanced Bitcoin's scalability and usability, addressing some of the concerns that initially hindered broader acceptance. Additionally, regulatory developments and institutional interest have introduced a new level of legitimacy to the market, encouraging traditional investors to enter the space. These changes are indicative of an evolving ecosystem that is increasingly responsive to market demands and user needs, reflecting a dynamic interplay between technological potential and economic realities.

As cryptocurrency adoption matures, its cultural impact becomes more pronounced. Satoshi Nakamoto's vision has inspired a diverse range of communities that share a common goal of redefining financial systems. The decentralized ethos has permeated various sectors, influencing discussions on privacy, ownership, and the role of technology in society. This cultural shift has led to a growing recognition of the ethical implications surrounding anonymity and decentralization, prompting ongoing debates about the responsibilities of users and developers in the cryptocurrency space. The landscape continues to evolve, driven by the foundational ideas put forth by Satoshi Nakamoto, making the future of cryptocurrency both promising and unpredictable.

Chapter 9: Satoshi Nakamoto and the Concept of Decentralization

Defining Decentralization

Decentralization is a foundational principle that distinguishes blockchain technology from traditional centralized systems. At its core, decentralization refers to the distribution of authority, responsibility, and control across a network rather than concentrating it in a single entity or a small group of entities. This concept is pivotal to the functioning of cryptocurrencies, as it empowers users by allowing them to engage directly with one another without the need for intermediaries. In the context of Bitcoin, Satoshi Nakamoto envisioned a financial system where trust is established through cryptographic proof rather than reliance on centralized institutions, thereby fostering a more inclusive and equitable economic landscape.

The implications of decentralization are profound, particularly in how it alters power dynamics in various sectors. In traditional finance, institutions like banks hold significant sway over transactions, often incurring fees and delays that can hinder accessibility. By contrast, decentralized networks enable peer-to-peer transactions, dramatically reducing costs and increasing transaction speeds. This shift not only democratizes financial services but also enhances security by minimizing single points of failure, making networks less vulnerable to systemic risks and fraud.

Satoshi Nakamoto's design for Bitcoin highlighted the importance of a decentralized ledger, where all participants in the network maintain a copy of the blockchain. This transparency is crucial for ensuring that all transactions are verifiable and tamper-proof, fostering trust among users. The role of miners in this system is equally significant; they validate transactions and contribute to network security through a competitive process. This decentralized consensus mechanism, known as proof-of-work, ensures that no single entity can control the network or manipulate the currency, reinforcing the integrity of the system.

Moreover, the philosophical implications of decentralization extend beyond mere functionality. Satoshi's anonymity serves as a statement against the conventional structures of power and control, reflecting a broader critique of centralized authorities. This philosophy resonates with various movements advocating for privacy, individual rights, and financial sovereignty. The emphasis on decentralization encourages users to take ownership of their assets and data, enabling a paradigm shift toward self-sovereignty that challenges traditional notions of authority and governance.

As the cryptocurrency landscape evolves, the concept of decentralization continues to be a focal point for discussions surrounding regulatory frameworks and ethical considerations. The tension between decentralized ideals and the need for oversight raises questions about the balance between innovation and security. Understanding decentralization in the context of Satoshi Nakamoto's vision allows for a deeper appreciation of its transformative potential and invites ongoing dialogue about its implications for the future of technology, finance, and society at large.

Satoshi's Vision for a Decentralized Economy

Satoshi Nakamoto's vision for a decentralized economy revolves around the fundamental principle of empowering individuals by removing intermediaries from financial transactions. This vision is encapsulated in the Bitcoin white paper, which articulates a peer-to-peer electronic cash system that enables direct transactions between users without the need for trusted third parties. By leveraging blockchain technology, Satoshi foresaw an economic model that not only enhances privacy and security but also democratizes access to financial services, allowing anyone with an internet connection to participate in the global economy.

At the core of Satoshi's philosophy is the belief in decentralization as a means to enhance individual autonomy and reduce the concentration of power. Traditional financial systems often require users to place trust in banks and centralized institutions, which can lead to systemic risks and potential abuse of power. Satoshi's proposal for a decentralized system shifts this trust from institutions to cryptographic proof, enabling users to verify transactions independently. This shift has profound implications, as it challenges the status quo of financial governance and proposes a model where individuals retain control over their own assets.

Satoshi's conception of a decentralized economy also addresses issues of censorship and inclusivity. In a traditional banking system, access is often restricted based on geographical location, socioeconomic status, or regulatory compliance. Satoshi envisioned a world where anyone could transact freely, regardless of their background or location. This aspect of his vision resonates particularly in regions with unstable financial systems or oppressive regimes, where individuals can leverage cryptocurrencies to bypass traditional barriers and maintain financial sovereignty.

Moreover, the historical context of Bitcoin's creation plays a crucial role in understanding Satoshi's vision. Emerging from the 2008 financial crisis, Bitcoin was conceived as a response to the failures of centralized financial institutions and the lack of accountability that characterized the global banking system. Satoshi's white paper not only proposed a technological solution but also served as a manifesto for a new economic paradigm, advocating for transparency, accountability, and a system that prioritizes the needs of individuals over institutions.

As Bitcoin and blockchain technology continue to evolve, the foundational principles set forth by Satoshi remain central to ongoing discussions about the future of finance. The decentralized economy envisioned by Satoshi has inspired a diverse array of projects and innovations that seek to further enhance user autonomy and redefine economic interactions. While the implementation of this vision faces numerous challenges, including regulatory scrutiny and technological hurdles, the pursuit of a decentralized economy continues to inspire a global movement that challenges traditional financial norms and promotes a more equitable economic landscape.

Challenges to Decentralization

Decentralization is often heralded as one of the foundational principles of blockchain technology, promising to disrupt traditional financial systems and empower users. However, the journey toward achieving true decentralization is fraught with significant challenges. One major obstacle is the concentration of mining power in the hands of a few large entities, which can lead to centralization of control over the network. This phenomenon is particularly evident in Bitcoin, where a handful of mining pools dominate the hash rate, raising concerns about the network's vulnerability to attacks and decision-making processes that may not reflect the interests of the broader community.

Another challenge to decentralization arises from the regulatory landscape that cryptocurrencies operate within. Governments around the world are grappling with how to regulate digital currencies, and their approaches can inadvertently promote centralization. For instance, compliance requirements often favor established players who can afford to navigate the complex legal frameworks, sidelining smaller, decentralized projects. The pressure for exchanges to implement know-your-customer (KYC) regulations can also lead to a centralization of user data, contradicting the privacy ideals that underpin many blockchain initiatives.

The technological infrastructure behind blockchain can also pose challenges to decentralization. While the concept of a distributed ledger is inherently decentralized, scalability issues can result in a reliance on centralized solutions to manage transaction throughput. High transaction fees and slower processing times during peak demand can push users toward centralized exchanges and custodial wallets, undermining the decentralized ethos. As blockchain networks grow, finding a balance between decentralization and efficiency remains a persistent hurdle.

Community governance is another critical area where challenges to decentralization manifest. The decision-making processes within blockchain projects often hinge on a small group of developers or stakeholders, which can lead to governance models that lack transparency and inclusivity. Disparities in knowledge and access to information can exacerbate this issue, creating a scenario where only a select few have the power to influence significant changes. This can result in a disconnect between the community's desires and the actions taken by those in positions of authority.

Finally, the cultural and ideological underpinnings of decentralization face scrutiny as cryptocurrencies gain mainstream attention. The initial vision espoused by Satoshi Nakamoto emphasized individual empowerment and community engagement, yet as digital currencies evolve, the market's focus has shifted toward profit and speculation. This transition can dilute the original goals of decentralization, leading to a culture that prioritizes short-term gains over long-term sustainability. As the ecosystem continues to mature, the challenge will be to reconcile these conflicting values while remaining true to the principles that inspired the creation of Bitcoin and other cryptocurrencies.

Chapter 10: Legal and Ethical Implications of Satoshi's Anonymity

Regulatory Perspectives

Regulatory perspectives on cryptocurrency are increasingly relevant as the technology evolves and matures. Governments and regulatory bodies worldwide grapple with how to manage the disruptive potential of blockchain technology while ensuring consumer protection and financial stability. This dynamic landscape is influenced significantly by the philosophies espoused in Satoshi Nakamoto's original white paper, where decentralization and autonomy were prioritized. The implications of these principles extend beyond the technology itself, challenging existing regulatory frameworks and creating a need for new policies that can accommodate innovative financial systems.

The anonymity of Satoshi Nakamoto presents a unique challenge for regulators. By remaining unidentified, Nakamoto has sparked numerous theories regarding the implications of anonymity in technology and finance. This aspect raises critical questions about accountability, liability, and the enforcement of laws in a decentralized environment. Regulators must consider how to approach entities and individuals who operate without a clear identity, complicating traditional methods of compliance and oversight. Consequently, the regulatory approach may require a nuanced understanding of the technological underpinnings of blockchain and the philosophical motivations of its early proponents.

Regulatory bodies often cite the need for consumer protection as a primary motivation for intervention in the cryptocurrency space. The volatility of digital assets, the potential for fraud, and the challenges of safeguarding user funds are significant concerns. The influence of Satoshi's white paper, which emphasized a peer-to-peer electronic cash system, complicates these discussions. As regulators seek to protect consumers from risks, they must also respect the foundational principles of decentralization and user empowerment that Nakamoto championed. This tension between regulation and innovation is at the heart of ongoing debates surrounding cryptocurrency policy.

The historical context of Bitcoin's creation further informs regulatory perspectives. Emerging from the 2008 financial crisis, Bitcoin was designed as an alternative to traditional financial systems, which many viewed as flawed and corrupt. This backdrop has led to a skeptical view of regulatory intervention, with proponents arguing that excessive regulation could stifle innovation and undermine the very principles that cryptocurrencies are built upon. As such, regulators must balance the need to mitigate risks with the necessity of fostering an environment conducive to technological advancement.

The cultural impact of Satoshi Nakamoto's work extends into the regulatory realm, influencing how different stakeholders perceive cryptocurrency. From tech enthusiasts to financial institutions, the narrative surrounding Nakamoto shapes attitudes toward regulation. As more entities seek to engage with cryptocurrency, regulators are faced with the complex task of developing frameworks that acknowledge this cultural shift while promoting responsible practices. Ultimately, the regulatory landscape will continue to evolve as stakeholders navigate the implications of Satoshi's legacy, balancing the innovative spirit of blockchain technology with the imperative of sound governance.

Ethical Considerations in Anonymity

Ethical considerations surrounding anonymity in the context of Satoshi Nakamoto's identity invoke a complex interplay between privacy, accountability, and trust within the cryptocurrency community. Nakamoto's decision to remain anonymous raises questions about the ethical implications of such a choice. On one hand, anonymity can protect individuals from persecution and allow for the free exchange of ideas. On the other hand, it can also create a lack of accountability, which can lead to potential misuse of the technology and its underlying principles. This duality highlights the need for a nuanced understanding of anonymity in the realm of cryptocurrency.

The ethical dimension of anonymity is particularly relevant when considering the impact of Satoshi's white paper on the development of blockchain technology. The white paper laid the groundwork for a decentralized financial system, advocating for transparency and trustless interactions. However, the very figure who championed these ideals chose to operate behind a veil of anonymity, raising questions about the integrity of these principles. Critics argue that without a known identity, it is challenging to hold Satoshi accountable for the consequences of the technology, especially as cryptocurrencies evolve and face regulatory scrutiny.

Moreover, the cultural impact of Satoshi Nakamoto's anonymity extends beyond technical considerations to influence societal perceptions of trust and authority. In a world where technology often seems centralized and controlled by a few entities, Nakamoto's choice to remain anonymous resonates with those who advocate for decentralization and empowerment of the individual. This cultural shift prompts discussions about the ethical responsibility of creators in the tech space, especially when their innovations can disrupt existing financial systems and societal norms.

Legal implications also arise from Satoshi's anonymity, as it complicates regulatory frameworks and the enforcement of laws surrounding cryptocurrencies. The absence of a known identity means that establishing liability in cases of fraud or market manipulation becomes challenging. This uncertainty can deter potential investors and users who may be wary of engaging with a system that lacks clear accountability. Ethical considerations thus extend into the realm of law, as the cryptocurrency community grapples with the potential need for a balance between innovation and the creation of a safe, trustworthy environment.

Ultimately, the legacy of Satoshi Nakamoto is intricately tied to the ethical implications of anonymity. While it serves as a shield for individual privacy and a catalyst for decentralized thought, it also raises critical questions about responsibility, trust, and the future of cryptocurrency. As the industry continues to evolve, it is essential for stakeholders to engage in ongoing discussions about the ethical ramifications of anonymity, ensuring that the foundational principles of blockchain technology remain intact while adapting to the challenges of a rapidly changing landscape.

The Future of Anonymity in Cryptocurrency

The future of anonymity in cryptocurrency is poised at a crucial intersection of technological advancement, regulatory scrutiny, and societal expectation. As blockchain technology evolves, the desire for privacy remains a contentious issue among users, developers, and regulators. The foundational principles laid out by Satoshi Nakamoto emphasized decentralization and pseudonymity, yet the growing demand for transparency and accountability in financial transactions has prompted debates over the necessity and viability of maintaining anonymity within the cryptocurrency ecosystem. The challenge will be to balance these competing interests while preserving the core values that define the cryptocurrency movement.

One of the significant factors influencing the future of anonymity is the development of privacy-centric cryptocurrencies. Coins like Monero, Zcash, and Dash employ advanced cryptographic techniques that allow users to transact without revealing their identities or transaction details. As regulatory bodies worldwide consider frameworks for cryptocurrency oversight, these privacy coins may face challenges related to compliance with anti-money laundering (AML) and know your customer (KYC) regulations. The outcome of these discussions will play a pivotal role in determining whether anonymity in cryptocurrency will be embraced or constrained by law.

Technological innovations such as zero-knowledge proofs and decentralized mixing services are also shaping the landscape of anonymity. These advancements offer enhanced privacy features that can obscure transaction trails while maintaining the integrity of the blockchain. However, their adoption raises concerns about potential misuse, as anonymity can facilitate illicit activities. Striking a balance between protecting user privacy and preventing criminal behavior will be crucial as developers work to enhance these technologies. The ongoing evolution of these tools will likely define a new paradigm for anonymity, one that may either reinforce Satoshi's vision or diverge significantly from it.

The cultural context surrounding cryptocurrency also influences the perception and future of anonymity. As digital currencies become more mainstream, public sentiment may shift towards greater acceptance of regulated anonymity. Users may advocate for their right to privacy, citing the importance of financial freedom and individual autonomy against state surveillance. This cultural push could lead to the formation of new social contracts within the cryptocurrency community, where the collective prioritizes anonymity as a fundamental right, reminiscent of the ideals championed by Satoshi Nakamoto during Bitcoin's inception.

Ultimately, the future of anonymity in cryptocurrency will depend on a complex interplay of technological advancements, regulatory frameworks, and cultural attitudes. As stakeholders navigate this landscape, they must consider the ethical implications of anonymity and the potential consequences of either excessive regulation or unregulated freedom. The legacy of Satoshi Nakamoto and the ideals embedded in Bitcoin's creation will serve as both a guiding light and a cautionary tale as the industry seeks to find a sustainable path forward that honors the principles of decentralization and privacy while addressing the legitimate concerns of broader society.

Chapter 11: The Cultural Impact of Satoshi Nakamoto on Tech and Finance

Bitcoin's Role in Financial Freedom

Bitcoin's emergence has been heralded as a transformative force in the quest for financial freedom. At its core, Bitcoin challenges traditional financial systems by decentralizing monetary control, allowing individuals to transact and store value without the need for intermediaries such as banks or governments. This shift empowers users to manage their own finances, thereby promoting autonomy and reducing reliance on established financial institutions that often impose fees and restrictions. As a result, Bitcoin serves as a tool for those seeking to escape the limitations and uncertainties of conventional banking systems.

The concept of financial freedom through Bitcoin is intricately linked to the principles of decentralization championed by Satoshi Nakamoto. By removing central authority, Bitcoin allows for peer-to-peer transactions that are transparent and secure, fostering an environment where users retain full control over their assets. This decentralization not only mitigates the risks associated with centralized financial systems, such as systemic failures and censorship, but also enhances privacy. Individuals can conduct transactions without revealing personal information, safeguarding their financial activities from prying eyes.

Moreover, Bitcoin offers a viable alternative for individuals in regions plagued by economic instability and hyperinflation. In countries where local currencies can swiftly lose value, Bitcoin provides a stable store of value that is immune to local economic policies. This resilience has enabled individuals to protect their wealth and engage in international trade without the hindrance of currency devaluation. Consequently, Bitcoin fosters a sense of security and hope, allowing individuals to navigate financial challenges with greater flexibility.

The impact of Satoshi Nakamoto's white paper cannot be overstated. It laid the groundwork for a new financial paradigm, inspiring a global movement towards decentralized finance. The ideas presented in the white paper resonate with those advocating for a financial system that prioritizes individual sovereignty over centralized control. As more people recognize the benefits of decentralization, the demand for Bitcoin and similar cryptocurrencies continues to grow, further solidifying their role in promoting financial independence.

Lastly, the ongoing evolution of Bitcoin post-Satoshi illustrates its adaptability and resilience as a financial instrument. The community of developers and advocates who continue to build upon Satoshi's vision ensures that Bitcoin remains relevant in a rapidly changing economic landscape. Innovations such as the Lightning Network enhance transaction efficiency, making Bitcoin a more practical option for everyday use. As Bitcoin matures, its potential to foster financial freedom expands, solidifying its place as a cornerstone of a new financial order, where individuals can reclaim control over their financial destinies.

Influence on Tech Startups and Innovation

The influence of Satoshi Nakamoto on tech startups and innovation is profound and multifaceted, reshaping not only the financial landscape but also the broader technology sector. The inception of Bitcoin represented a radical departure from traditional financial systems, inspiring a new generation of entrepreneurs to explore decentralized models. This shift has led to the emergence of numerous startups that leverage blockchain technology to provide innovative solutions across various sectors, including finance, supply chain, healthcare, and more. By proposing a system that operates without intermediaries, Nakamoto's vision has encouraged startups to think outside the conventional frameworks, fostering a culture of experimentation and disruption.

Nakamoto's white paper laid the groundwork for a plethora of blockchain-based innovations. The principles of decentralization, transparency, and security outlined in the document have become foundational to countless projects. For instance, the rise of decentralized finance (DeFi) platforms directly stems from the desire to replicate and enhance the functionalities of traditional banking systems without the associated risks of central control. Startups are now exploring ways to create decentralized applications (dApps) that empower users, reflecting Nakamoto's ethos of putting power back into the hands of individuals rather than centralized authorities.

The anonymity of Satoshi Nakamoto has also played a crucial role in shaping the culture of innovation within the tech startup ecosystem. By remaining unseen, Nakamoto has become a symbol of the potential of decentralized technologies to operate independently of individual influence or control. This has encouraged many founders to prioritize their projects over personal branding, fostering a collaborative environment where ideas can flourish without the constraints of hierarchical structures. The focus on community-driven development rather than individual acclaim has allowed for a diverse range of voices and perspectives to contribute to the evolution of blockchain technology.

Furthermore, Satoshi's communication style and online presence have significantly influenced how startups interact with their communities. Nakamoto's early engagement with users on forums and mailing lists established a model of transparency and open dialogue that many tech startups have adopted. This approach has led to the creation of vibrant communities around projects, where feedback and collaboration are encouraged. Startups are now more likely to involve their users in the development process, leading to products that are better aligned with the needs and desires of their target audience.

In the context of legal and ethical implications, Satoshi's legacy poses both challenges and opportunities for tech startups. The decentralized nature of blockchain technology raises questions about regulation, security, and the ethical responsibilities of developers.

Startups must navigate these complexities while remaining true to the principles of decentralization that Nakamoto championed. As the industry matures, the influence of Satoshi Nakamoto will continue to be felt, inspiring innovation while also prompting critical discussions about the balance between autonomy and accountability in the tech landscape.

Satoshi's Legacy in Popular Culture

Satoshi Nakamoto's influence extends far beyond the confines of the cryptocurrency realm, permeating various aspects of popular culture. The enigma surrounding Nakamoto's true identity has sparked a myriad of theories and narratives, captivating the imaginations of writers, filmmakers, and artists. This intrigue has given rise to a plethora of books, documentaries, and even fictional portrayals that explore the mystery of Satoshi, often blending fact with speculation. The cultural fascination with Nakamoto underscores not only the significance of Bitcoin but also the larger themes of anonymity and innovation in the digital age.

In literature, Nakamoto's story has inspired a range of works that delve into the implications of decentralized technology. Authors have explored the philosophical and ethical dilemmas posed by a pseudonymous creator, reflecting on how anonymity can be both a shield and a weapon in the digital landscape. These narratives often highlight the tension between the idealism of Satoshi's vision and the practical realities of cryptocurrency's impact on society. This thematic exploration resonates with a broader audience, inviting readers to consider the implications of technology on trust, identity, and power structures.

Film and television have also embraced Satoshi's legacy, with several productions attempting to dramatize the mystery surrounding the figure. Documentaries have sought to unravel the enigma, presenting interviews with key players in the cryptocurrency space and examining the cultural impact of Bitcoin. Fictional representations often portray Satoshi as a modern-day Robin Hood or a reclusive genius, reflecting society's fascination with the archetype of the misunderstood innovator. These portrayals contribute to the mythos of Nakamoto, elevating the figure to a near-mythical status within the cultural zeitgeist.

Moreover, Satoshi's legacy has influenced the music industry, with artists referencing Bitcoin and Nakamoto in their lyrics and works. This intersection of cryptocurrency and pop music signifies a broader acceptance and integration of blockchain concepts into mainstream culture. Musicians have begun to explore themes of decentralization, financial freedom, and the disruptive potential of technology, echoing the ideals that Nakamoto championed. These artistic expressions not only celebrate the innovations sparked by Bitcoin but also serve as a vehicle for broader discussions about the future of finance and individual empowerment.

Ultimately, Satoshi Nakamoto's legacy in popular culture reflects a complex interplay of fascination, speculation, and inspiration. The reverberations of Nakamoto's work continue to shape narratives across various media, encouraging a global dialogue about the implications of cryptocurrency and blockchain technology. As Satoshi's story unfolds, it remains a testament to the enduring allure of anonymity and the transformative potential of decentralized systems in our increasingly digital world. The cultural impact of Satoshi Nakamoto exemplifies how technology can inspire creativity and provoke critical thought, solidifying Nakamoto's role as a pivotal figure in both tech and finance.

www.ingramcontent.com/pod-product-compliance
Lightning Source LLC
Chambersburg PA
CBHW040240220526
45473CB00001B/316